Animal Peculiarity Part 3

By T.P Just

~~~

Copyright © 2010 by Terence Just. All rights reserved.

This eBook is licensed for your personal enjoyment only. This eBook may not be re-sold or given away to other people. If you would like to share this book with another person, please purchase an additional copy for each recipient.

Get All The Books In The Series:

Animal Peculiarity Part 1
Animal Peculiarity Part 2
Animal Peculiarity Part 3
Animal Peculiarity Part 4
Animal Peculiarity Part 5
Animal Peculiarity Part 6
Animal Peculiarity Part 7
Animal Peculiarity Part 8
Just Enterprises

Table of Contents

1 Prologue

THERE is perhaps nothing extraordinary in the fact that man is wise and just, takes great care to provide for his own children, -shows due consideration for his parents, seeks sustenance for himself, protects himself against plots, and possesses all the other gifts of nature which are his. For man has been endowed with speech, of all things the most precious, and has been granted reason, which is of the greatest help and use.

Moreover, he knows how to reverence and worship the gods. But that dumb animals should by nature possess some good quality and should have many of man's amazing excellences assigned to them along with man, is indeed a remarkable fact. And to know accurately the special characteristics of each, and how living creatures also have been a source of interest no less than man, demands a trained intelligence and much learning. Now I am well aware of the labour that others have expended on this subject, yet I have collected all the materials that I could; I have clothed them in untechnical language, and am persuaded that my achievement is a treasure far from negligible. So if anyone considers them profitable, let him make use of them; anyone who does not consider them so may give them to his father to keep and attend to.

For not all things give pleasure to all men, nor do all men consider all subjects worthy of study. Although I was born later than many accomplished writers of an earlier day, the accident of date ought not to mulct me of praise, if I too produce a learned work whose ampler research and whose choice of language make it deserving of serious attention.

2 Basse and Prawn

The Basse is a victim of the Prawn and is inclined to be (if I may be allowed the jest) the greatest gourmet among fish. So being lake dwellers they lie in wait for the lake Prawns. These are of three kinds: the first are such as I have already mentioned; the second subsist on seaweed, while the third kind live on the rocks.

Being incapable of self-defence against the Basse, they prefer to die along with it; and I shall not hesitate to use the word 'stratagem' of them. For instance, directly they realise that they are being caught, these precious creatures adroitly turn outwards the projecting portion of their head, which resembles the beak of a trireme and is exceedingly sharp and has moreover notches in it like a saw, and spring and leap lightly and nimbly about.

But the Basse opens its mouth wide, and the flesh of its throat is tender. So the Basse seizes the exhausted Prawn and fancies that, it is going to make a meal of it. The Prawn however in this ample space gambols about and a dance in triumph, so to say, over the Basses throat.

Then it plants its spikes in their unfortunate pursuers, whose inward parts are thereby lacerated, so that they swell up and discharge much blood and choke the Basse, until in most novel fashion the slayer is himself slain.

3 The Porcupine

Strength of claws and sharpness of fangs make bears, wolves, leopards, and lions bold, whereas the Porcupine, which (I am told) has not these advantages, none the less has not been left by Nature destitute of weapons wherewith to defend itself. For instance, against those who would attack it with intent to harm it discharges the hairs on its body, like javelins, and raising the bristles on its back, frequently makes a good shot. And these hairs leap forth as though sped from a bowstring.

4 Mutual hatred of Moray, Octopus and Crayfish

Enmity and inborn hate are a truly terrible Mutual affliction and a cruel disease when once they have sunk deep into the heart even of brute beasts, and nothing can purge them away. For instance, the Moray loathes the Octopus, and the Octopus is the enemy of the Crayfish, and to the Moray the Cray—fish is most hostile.

Moray and Octopus

The Moray with its sharp teeth cuts through the tentacles of the Octopus, and then boring into its stomach does the same thing and very properly, for the Moray swims, while the Octopus is like some creeping thing. And even though it changes its colour to that of the rocks, even this artifice seems to avail it nothing, for the Moray is quick to perceive the creature's stratagem.

Octopus and Crayfish

As to the Crayfish, the Octopuses strangle them with their grip, and when they have succeeded in killing them, they suck out their flesh. But against the Moray the Crayfish raises its horns and with fury in them challenges it.

Moray and Crayfish

Thereupon the Moray imprudently tries to bite the prickles which its adversary has thrust forward in self-defence. But the Crayfish reaches out its claws like two hands, clinging firmly to the Moray's throat on either side, never relaxes its hold, while the Moray in its distress writhes and transfixes itself on the points of the Cray fish's shell; and as these are planted in it, it grows numb and gives up the struggle, finally sinking in exhaustion. And the Crayfish makes a meal off its adversary.

The Moray

The fish known as the Moray lives in the sea, and when the net encircles it, it swims hither and thither, seeking with great cleverness some weak mesh or some rent in the net. And when it has found such a place, it slips through and swims free once again. And if one of them has this good fortune, all the others of its kind that have been caught will, along with it escape in the same way, as though taking their direction from a leader.

The Cuttlefish

Whenever fishermen who are skilled in these matters plan to catch a Cuttlefish, the fish on realising this emits the ink from its body, pours it over itself and envelops itself so as to be entirely invisible. The fisherman's sight is deceived though the fish is within view, he does not see it. It was by veiling Aeneas in such a cloud that Poseidon tricked Achilles, according to Homer.

5 Birds and their protection against sorcery

Even brute beasts protect themselves against the eyes of sorcerers and wizards by some inexplicable and marvelous gift of Nature. For instance, I am told that as a charm against sorcery ring-doves, nibble off the fine shoots of the bay-tree, and then insert them in their nests as a protection for their young.

Kites take buck-thorn, falcons picris, while turtle-doves take the fruit of the iris, ravens the agnus-castus tree, but hoopoes maidenhair fern, which some call ' lovely hair'; the crow takes vervain, the shearwater ivy, the heron a crab, the touch from the bats turns them to wind-eggs and makes them infertile. Accordingly, this is the remedy they use to prevent this happening.

They lay the leaves of a plane-tree upon their nests, and directly the bats come near the storks, they are benumbed and become incapable of doing harm. On swallows too Nature has bestowed a like gift: cockroaches injure their eggs. Therefore the mother-birds protect their chicks with celery leaves, and hence the cockroaches cannot reach them.

6 Effect of certain herbs on fish and reptiles

If one throws some rue upon an octopus it remains immobile-
so the story goes. If you touch a snake with a reed, it will after
the first stroke remain still, and in the grip of numbness will
lie quiet; if however you repeat the stroke a second or a third
time, you at once revive its strength.

The moray too, if struck once with a fennel wand, lies still the
first time, but if struck several times, its anger is kindled.

Fisher folk assert that even octopuses come ashore if a sprig of
olive is laid upon the beach.

7 Elephant's fat

It seems that the fat of an elephant is a remedy against the poisons of all savage creatures, and if a man rubs some on his body, even though he encounter unarmed the very fiercest, he will escape unscathed.

The Elephant, fond of perfumes

The Elephant has at terror of a horned ram and of the squealing of a pig. It was by these means, they say, that the Romans turned to flight the Perfumes elephants of Pyrrhus of Epirus, and that the. Romans won a glorious victory.
This same animal is over-come by beauty in a woman and lays aside its temper, quite stunned by the lovely sight. And at Alexandria in Egypt, they say, an Elephant was the rival of Aristophanes of Byzantium for the love of a woman who was engaged in making garlands. The Elephant also loves every kind of fragrance and is fascinated by the scent of perfumes and of flowers.

8 How to stop dogs barking

If some thief or robber wants to silence dogs that are too fierce
and to make them run away, he takes a brand from a funeral
pyre (they say) and goes for them. The dogs are terrified.
I have heard too this story: if a man shears a sheep that has
been mauled by a wolf, and after working the wool makes
himself a tunic, this will irritate him so when he puts it on.

Wool as irritant

He is weaving a gnawing itch for himself, as the proverb has
it.

Quarrel at a dinner-party

If a man wants to bring about a quarrel and contention at a
dinner-party, he will by dropping into the wine a stone that a
dog has bitten, vex his fellow-guests to the point of frenzy.

Scents pleasant and unpleasant

If a man sprinkle some perfume upon beetles, Scents which are ill-smelling creatures, they cannot endure the sweet scent, but die. In the same way it is said that tanners, who live all their life in foul air, detest perfumes. And the Egyptians maintain that all snakes dread the feathers of the ibis.

9 The Sting-ray, how caught

Those who have a thorough understanding of the matter hunt Sting-rays, and it is chiefly in this way that their efforts are successful. They take their stand and dance and sing very sweetly.

And the Sting-rays are soothed by the sound and are charmed by the dancing and draw nearer, while the men with- draw gently step by step to the spot where of course - the snare is set for the wretched creatures, namely nets spread out. Then the Sting-rays fall into them and are caught, betrayed in the first instance by the dancing and singing.

The Sting-ray

The barb of the Sting-ray nothing can withstand. It wounds and kills instantly, and even those fishermen who have great knowledge of the sea dread its weapon, for no man can heal the wound, nor will the creature, that inflicted it; that was a gift vouchsafed, most probably, to the ashen spear from Mount Pelion alone!

10 The Great Tunney

The Great Tunney, as it is called, is a monstrous fish and knows well what is best for it. This gift it has acquired by nature and not by art. For instance, when the hook has pierced it, it dives to the bottom and thrusts and dashes itself against the ground, striking its mouth in its effort to eject the hook. If that fails, it widens the wound and disgorges the instrument of pain and dashes away. Frequently however it fails in the attempt and the fisherman draws up the reluctant creature and secures his catch.

11 The Melanurus (black-tail)

The Melanurus is the most timid of fishes and to its timidity fishermen bear witness, for it is not caught in weels nor does it go near them; but if by chance a dragnet encircles it, then it is caught without knowing it.

And whenever the sea is fairly calm and smooth, these fish lie quiet down below upon the rocks or among the seaweed and cover themselves as best they can, trying to conceal their bodies. But if the weather is stormy, observing other fish diving to the depths out of the buffeting waves, they take courage and approach the shore, swim close to the rocks, and fancy that the foam heating overhead is sufficient protection while it conceals and overshadows them.

And they know in some quite inexplicable way that for fishermen the sea is unnavigable on such a day or such a night, as it rages with the waves mounting to a terrifying height. It is in stormy weather that they gather their food, when the swell drags some off the rocks and sucks some from the shore.

The Melanuruses feed off the foulest matter, such stuff as no other fish would readily take, unless it were utterly overcome by hunger. But in calm weather they have only the sand to ride on, and from there they get their food. But how they are captured another shall tell.

12 The Eagle, its keen sight

Among birds the Eagle has the keenest sight. And Homer is aware of this and testifies to the fact in the story of Patroclus when he compares Menelaus to the bird at the time when he was searching for Antilochus, that he might dispatch him to Achilles as a messenger, unwelcome indeed but necessary, to announce the fate that had be fallen his comrade, whom Achilles had sent out to battle) but never welcomed home again for all his yearning.

And the Eagle is said to serve not him-self alone but to be good for men's eyes as well. At any rate, if a man whose sight is dim mix an Eagle's gall with Attic honey and rub it (on his eyes), he will see and will acquire sight of extreme keenness.

13 The Nightingale

Among birds the Nightingale has the clearest and most musical voice, and fills solitary places with its most lovely and thrilling note. Further, they say that its flesh is good for keeping one awake. But people who feast upon such food are evil and dreadfully foolish. And it is an evil attribute of a food that it drives away sleep, the king of gods and men, as Homer says.

The Crane

The screaming of Cranes brings on showers, so they say, while their brain possesses some kind of spell that leads women to grant sexual favours, if those who first observed the fact are sufficient guarantee.

Vulture's feathers

If a man burn the feathers of a Vulture (so I am told), he will have no difficulty in inducing snakes to quit their dens and lurking-places.

14 The Woodpecker

The bird 'Woodpecker' derives its name from what it does. For it has a curved beak with which it pecks oak-trees, and deposits its young in them as in a nest; and it has no need at all of dry twigs woven together or of any building.

Now if one inserts a stone and blocks up the entrance for the aforesaid bird, it guesses that there is a plot afoot, fetches some herb that is obnoxious to the stone, and places it against the stone. The latter in disgust and unable to endure (the smell) springs out, and once again the bird's caverned home lies open to it.

15 The Four-toothed Sparus

The Four-toothed Sparus is not solitary nor does it endure
loneliness and separation from its kind. These fish love to
congregate together according to their age: the younger ones
swim about in shoals the matured ones also keep together.
And as the saying is true a friend must be of one's own age, so
these creatures delight to be where others of their kind are,
like comrades and friends sharing the same pursuits- and
resorts. And these are the means they devise for evading their
pursuers.
Whenever an angler drops a bait for them: they all gather
round and forming a ring look at one another as though each
were signaling to each not to approach and not to touch the
bait that has been lowered.

And those that have been posted for this purpose remain still. But a Sparus from some other, strange shoal arrives and swallows the bait and gets the reward of its solitariness by being caught. So while he is being drawn up, the rest grow bolder as though they were not going to be taken, and so through their scorn (of danger) are caught.

16 The Raven, its thirst

All through the summer the Raven afflicted with a parching thirst, and with his croaking (so they say) declares his punishment. And the reason they give is this. Being a servant he was sent out by Apollo to draw water.

He came to a field of corn, tall but still green, and waited till it should ripen as he wanted to nibble the wheat: to his master's orders he paid no heed. On that account in the driest season of the year he is punished with thirst. This looks like a fable, but let me repeat it out of reverence for the god.

The Raven, in divination

The Raven, they say, is a sacred bird and attends upon Apollo: that is why men agree that nation it is also of use in divination, and those who understand the positions of birds, their cries, and their flight whether on the left or on the right hand, are able to divine by its croaking.

Its eggs

I am also informed that Raven's eggs turn the hair black. And it is essential for anyone who is dyeing his hair to keep olive oil in his mouth and his lips closed. Otherwise his teeth also turn black along with his hair, and they are hardly to be washed white again.

17 Moray and Viper

Whenever the Moray is filled with amorous impulses it comes out of the sea on to land seeking eagerly for a mate, and a very evil mate.

For it goes to a Viper's den and the pair embrace. And they do say that the male Viper also in its frenzied desire for copulation goes down to the sea, and just as a reveler with his flute knocks at the door, so the Viper also with his hissing summons his loved one and she emerges.

Thus does Nature bring those that dwell far apart together in a mutual desire and to a common bed.

The Bee-eater

The Bee-eater flies (so they say) in precisely the opposite way to all other birds, for they move forward in the direction in which they look, while the Bee-eater flies backwards. And I am astonished at the remarkable, incredible, and uncommon character of the motion with which this creature wings its way.

18 Snakes, how generated

The spine of a dead man they say, transforms the putrefying marrow into a snake. The brute emerges, and from the gentlest of beings crawls forth the fiercest. Now the remains of those that were fine and noble are at rest and their reward is peace, even as the soul also of such men has the rewards which wise men celebrate in their songs.

But it is from the spine of evildoers that such evil monsters are begotten even after life. The fact is, the whole story is either a fable, or if it is to be relied upon as true, then the corpse of a wicked man receives (so I think) the reward of his ways in becoming the progenitor of a snake.

19 The Swallow

A Swallow is a sign that the best season of the year is at hand.
And it is friendly to man and takes a pleasure in sharing the
same roof with this being.
It comes uninvited, and when it pleases and sees fit, it departs.
Men welcome it in accordance with the law of hospitality laid
down by Homer who bids us cherish a guest while he is with
us and speed him on his way when he wishes to leave.

20 The Goat, its breathing

The Goat has a certain advantage (over other animals) in the manner of taking breath, as the narratives of shepherds tell us, for it inhales through its ears as well was through its nostrils, and has a sharper perception than any other cloven-hoofed animal.

The cause of this I am unable to tell; I have only told what I know. But if the Goat also was a creation of Prometheus, what the intention of this contrivance was, I leave, him to determine.

21 Poisonous Snakes

They say that the bite of the Viper and of other snakes is not without countering remedies. Some, I am told, are to be drunk, others are to be applied; spells too can mitigate poison injected by a sting.

But the bite of the Asp alone, I am told, cannot be cured and is beyond help. This creature truly deserves to be hated for being blessed with the power to injure.

Yet a monster more abominable and harder to avoid even than the Asp is a sorceress, such as (we are told) Medea and Circe were, for the poison from Asps is the result of a bite, whereas sorceresses kill by a mere touch, so they say.

22 The Dog-Fish

Those that are speckled one may call galeus (small shark), and the rest, if you call them Spiny Dog-fish you will not go far wrong. Now the speckled ones have a softer skin and a flatter head, while the others, whose skin is hard and whose head tapers to a point, are distinguished from the rest by the whiteness of their skin.

Moreover nature has provided them with spines, one on their crest, so to say, the other in the tail. And these spines are hard and resisting and emit a kind of poison. Of the small Dog-fish both kinds are caught in the ooze and mud, and the manner of catching them I may as well explain. By way of bait men let down a white fish out of which they have out the backbone. Directly one of the Dog-fish is caught and hooked, all those that have seen make a- rush for him and follow him as he is drawn upwards, never stopping until they reach the boat. One might imagine that they do this out of envy, as though he had filched some piece of food from somewhere and all for himself. And it often happens that some of them actually leap into the boat and are caught of their own free will.

The Shark

There are three kinds of Sea-hound. The first is of enormous size and may be reckoned among the most daring of sea monsters. The others are of two kinds; they live in the mud and reach to a cubit in length.

Get All The Books In The Series:

Animal Peculiarity Part 1
Animal Peculiarity Part 2
Animal Peculiarity Part 3
Animal Peculiarity Part 4
Animal Peculiarity Part 5
Animal Peculiarity Part 6
Animal Peculiarity Part 7
Animal Peculiarity Part 8